Mama,
How Does The Wind
Start To Blow?

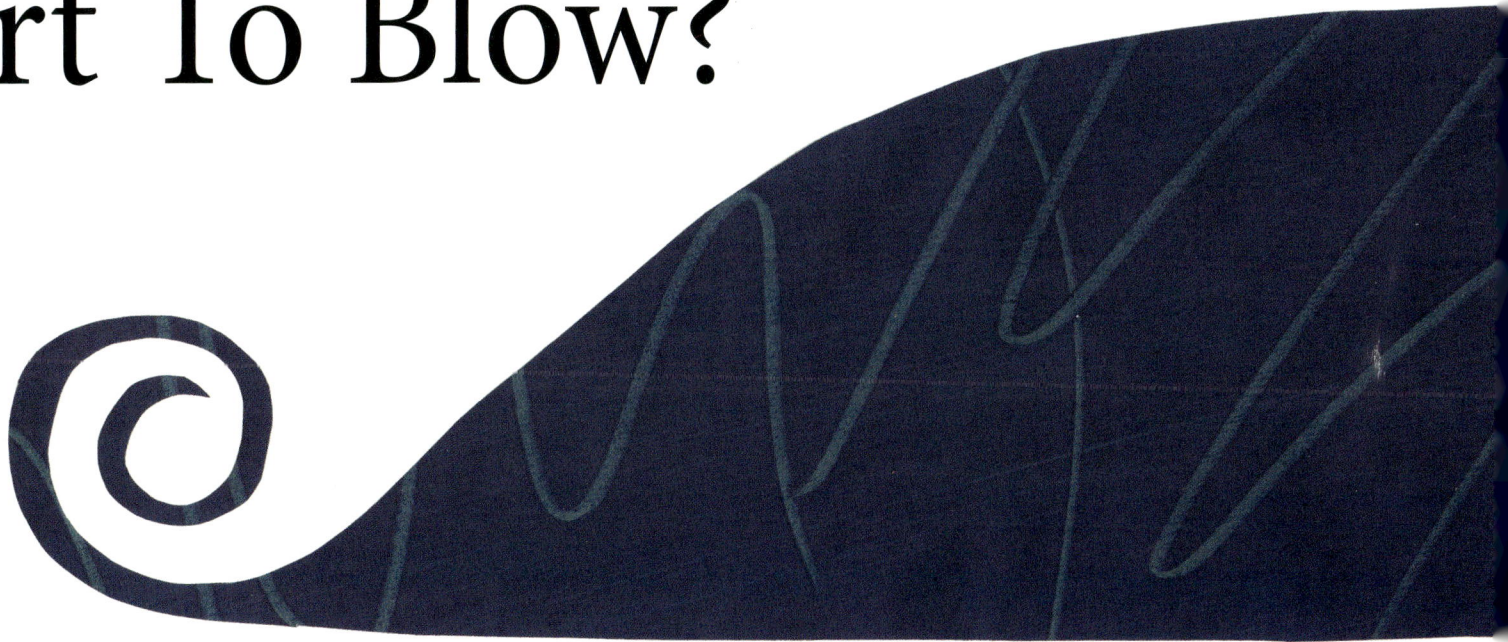

Dedicated to
Anthony, Andrea, Kayla, and Elizabeth
You will always feel my wind on your face.

ISBN # 978-0-9910946-3-9

Printed in the United States of America
by Worzalla, 3535 Jefferson Street, Stevens Point, Wisconsin

I would like to thank, thank, thank, Lindsay for all her creative talent in helping me publish my first book! www.lindsaylindnerdesign@gmail.com

Published by
JeanneKay Publishing
For information about the author and ordering please contact:
website: www.mrsjeanne.com   email: hello@mrsjeanne.com

Revison 3

Mama, How Does The Wind Start To Blow?

A Counting Story That Will Blow You Away!

Written and Illustrated by Jeanne Styczinski

Mama, I want to know.

How does the wind start to blow?

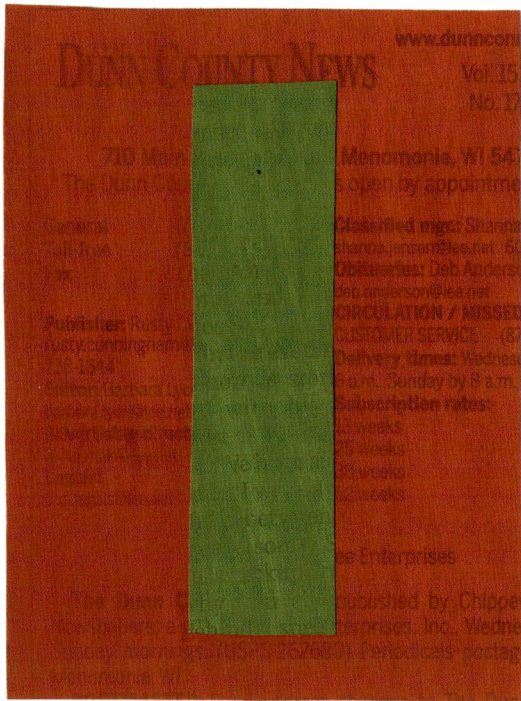

Does wind start when the moon begins to rise?

No, wind doesn't start when the moon begins to rise.
Wind doesn't start that way!

2

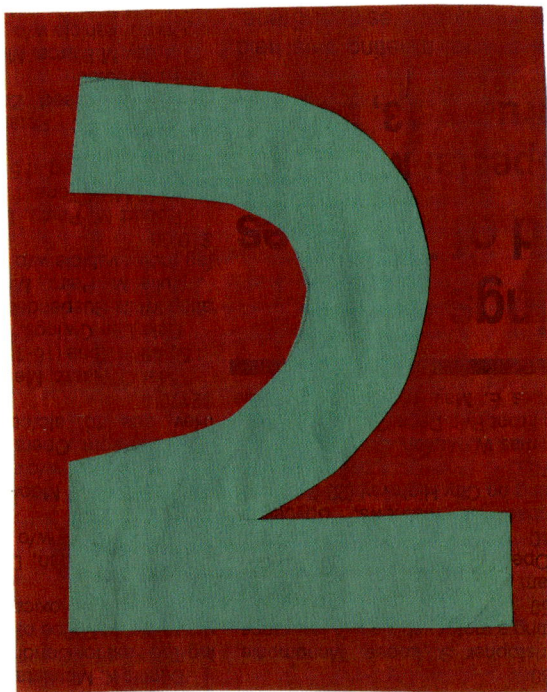

Does wind start when two stars fall from the sky?

No, wind doesn't start when two stars fall from the sky.
Wind doesn't start that way!

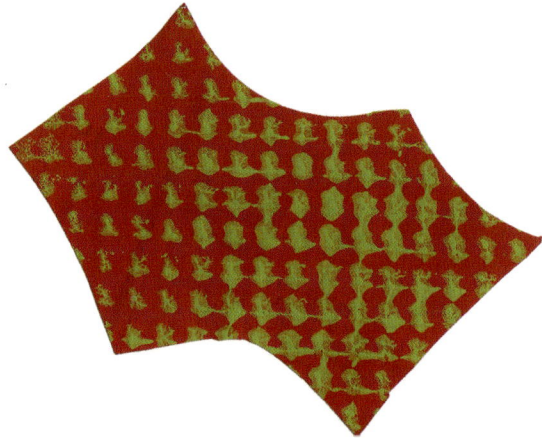

Does wind start when three leaves fall from a tree?

No, wind doesn't start when three leaves fall from a tree. Wind doesn't start that way!

Does wind start when four horses start to swish their tails?

No, wind doesn't start when four horses start to swish their tails.
Wind doesn't start that way!

Does wind start when five owls hoot from a branch high in a tree?

No, wind doesn't start when five owls hoot from a branch high in a tree.
Wind doesn't start that way!

6

Does wind start when six fireflies blink in the night?

No, wind doesn't start when six fireflies blink in the night.
Wind doesn't start that way!

7

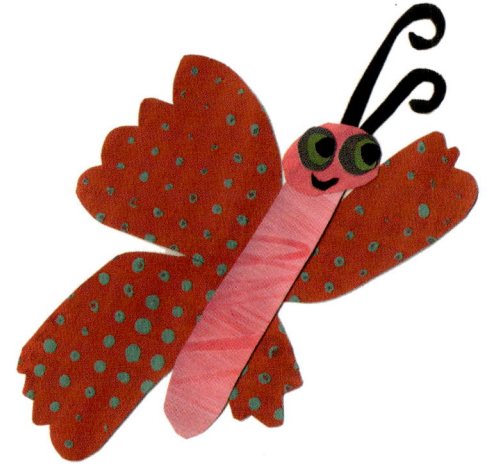

Does wind start when seven butterflies flutter their wings?

No, wind doesn't start when seven butterflies flutter their wings. Wind doesn't start that way!

8

Does wind start when eight bees start to buzz really loud?

No, wind doesn't start when eight bees start to buzz really loud.
Wind doesn't start that way!

9

Does wind start when nine frogs leap off a pink lily pad?

No, wind doesn't start when nine frogs leap off a pink lily pad. Wind doesn't start that way!

10

Does wind start when ten seeds fall from a flower so tall?

No, wind doesn't start when ten seeds fall from a flower so tall.
Wind doesn't start that way!
Then how? How does the wind start to blow?

It's simple.

Wind starts when a Mother blows an, **"I Love You"** kiss to her child.

Like this!

Catch it! This wind is for you! Catch it! This wind is for you!

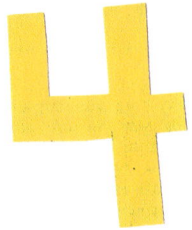    

6

7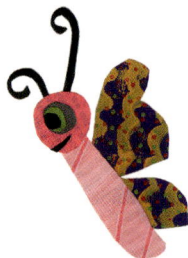

8

9

10

Got Wind?

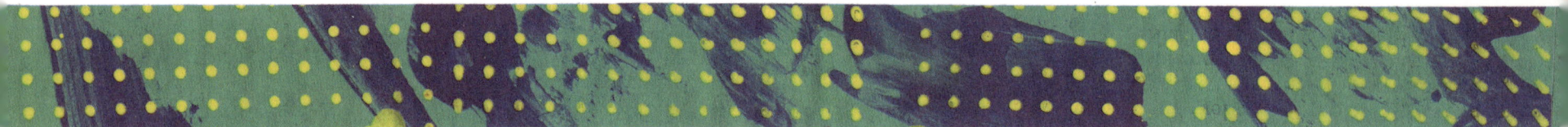

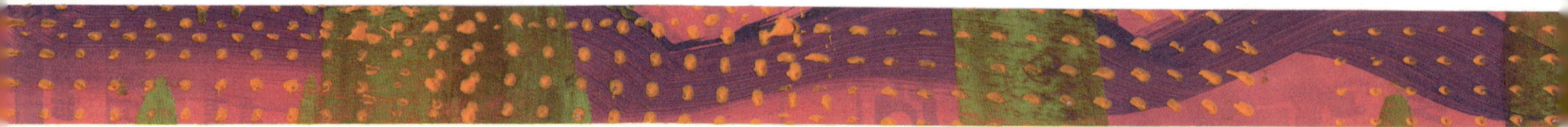

Washington Road
WI 53212
5110
Gray
Attorne

centers
we're still growing!
We offer:

Oven H   from 2-3 pm
3 bedroo   downtown
Shell lake   private se
                                kitchen ba

half-naked
the wreckage
                                give me
                                of State Emp

WI 54612

MUST UNDERSTAND ENGLISH
FLUENT ENGLISH